Assessing Misperceptions Online About the Security Clearance Process

MAREK N. POSARD, SINA BEAGHLEY, HAMAD AL-IBRAHIM,
EMILY ELLINGER

Prepared for the Performance Accountability Council Program
Management Office
Approved for public release; distribution unlimited

NATIONAL DEFENSE RESEARCH INSTITUTE

T0002908

For more information on this publication, visit **www.rand.org/t/RRA1690-1**.

About RAND

The RAND Corporation is a research organization that develops solutions to public policy challenges to help make communities throughout the world safer and more secure, healthier and more prosperous. RAND is nonprofit, nonpartisan, and committed to the public interest. To learn more about RAND, visit www.rand.org.

Research Integrity

Our mission to help improve policy and decisionmaking through research and analysis is enabled through our core values of quality and objectivity and our unwavering commitment to the highest level of integrity and ethical behavior. To help ensure our research and analysis are rigorous, objective, and nonpartisan, we subject our research publications to a robust and exacting quality-assurance process; avoid both the appearance and reality of financial and other conflicts of interest through staff training, project screening, and a policy of mandatory disclosure; and pursue transparency in our research engagements through our commitment to the open publication of our research findings and recommendations, disclosure of the source of funding of published research, and policies to ensure intellectual independence. For more information, visit www.rand.org/about/research-integrity.

RAND's publications do not necessarily reflect the opinions of its research clients and sponsors.

Published by the RAND Corporation, Santa Monica, Calif.
© 2023 RAND Corporation
RAND® is a registered trademark.

Library of Congress Cataloging-in-Publication Data is available for this publication.

ISBN: 978-1-9774-1030-6

Cover: PeopleImages/Getty Images.

About This Report

The purpose of this report is to describe and analyze information and potential misinformation available online about the security clearance process, which could lead to misperceptions about the process. Some applicants may find this process confusing and opaque, leading them to seek out clarification from acquaintances, friends, and family members, in person or online. Much of this online information is publicly available and can give the government insights into what topics people are concerned about regarding the security clearance process and what information is available to those individuals from both official and nonofficial sources.

The research reported here was completed on September 30, 2022, and underwent security review with the sponsor and the Defense Office of Prepublication and Security Review before public release.

National Security Research Division

This research was sponsored by the Security, Suitability, and Credentialing Performance Accountability Council Program Management Office and conducted within the Personnel, Readiness, and Health Program of the RAND National Security Research Division (NSRD), which operates the National Defense Research Institute (NDRI), a federally funded research and development program sponsored by the Office of the Secretary of Defense, the Joint Staff, the Unified Combatant Commands, the Navy, the Marine Corps, the defense agencies, and the defense intelligence enterprise.

For more information on the RAND Personnel, Readiness, and Health Program, see www.rand.org/nsrd/prh or contact the director (contact information is provided on the webpage).

Acknowledgments

We would like to thank our sponsor, the Performance Accountability Council Program Management Office. David Colangelo, Renee Oberlin, Travis Furman, and Heather Clawson were particularly helpful throughout the course of the project. We are grateful to Sydne Newberry for her help in improving the prose of this report. Finally, we thank Benjamin Miller and Adam Lurie for their thoughtful reviews on earlier drafts of this report.

Summary

The purpose of this report is to describe and analyze information and potential misinformation available online about the security clearance process that could lead to misperceptions about the process. The security clearance process may seem confusing and opaque to the public, leading some people to seek clarity from others about their own experiences. Seeking out this kind of information from acquaintances, friends, and family is nothing new, but access to the internet allows people to search for additional sources that might offer answers to their questions, as well as inquire of a larger number of people on public forums about this process. Reviewing the questions and content on such forums provides insight into what people are asking—and what answers they are getting—and reveals areas in which there are potential misperceptions about the process.

The Performance Accountability Council Program Management Office asked RAND's National Security Research Division to assess online information about the security clearance process, in particular information that may lead some people to misperceive this process. To this end, this report was designed to answer two questions:

1. What types of information about the security clearance process are online?
2. Where are opportunities to clarify areas of confusion about the clearance process?

The report presents results from a qualitative analysis of select online content, as well as results from an automated topic model that identified key themes from select online forums that focus on discussions about the clearance process. We found that government sources were comprehensive but more difficult to understand versus nongovernment sources. Furthermore, we found that most nongovernment information online was not necessarily false but could lead to misperceptions. Finally, we identified popular topics discussed in online forums that could lead to misperceptions by some users. We recommend that the government develop and release more-accessible information, periodically assess online information to understand potential misperceptions, consider targeted outreach, and evaluate the effectiveness of these outreach methods.

Contents

Figure and Tables

Figure

Tables

Introduction

The purpose of this report is to describe and analyze the information and misinformation that people share online about the security clearance process that could lead to misperceptions about the process. We define *misinformation* as false information that is not intended to cause harm.[1] Further, we define *misperceptions* as beliefs that are partially or completely false.[2]

With the growth of internet access, potential applicants are likely to seek out information online about the security clearance process. Such information may include official and unofficial sources, as well as information from anonymous users on social media. Seeking out information from other people about these experiences is nothing new—people often ask acquaintances, friends, and family for input about something they may not understand.[3]

What is new, however, is that there are more people online sharing their anecdotal experiences. Many of these conversations exist in publicly accessible venues, making them available for review. These conversations can help inform outreach efforts by the government to help the public understand how the clearance process works. To that end, this report was designed to answer two questions:

1. What types of information about the security clearance process are online?
2. Where are opportunities for the government to clarify areas of confusion about the clearance process?

Chapter 1 presents some of the reasons why there could be confusion about the security clearance process; we continue with a discussion about the potential consequences for this confusion and then outline the rest of this report.

The Security Clearance Process

Once a job candidate is conditionally hired for a position that requires a security clearance, the individual will have to begin the background investigation process. The first major step in that process is for the individual to fill out and submit the *Questionnaire for National Security Positions* (the Standard Form [SF]-86),[4] which is currently a lengthy form requesting detailed information from the applicant, including where they have lived and worked, foreign travel, foreign contacts, drug and alcohol use, and organizational affiliations. The U.S. government assumes that all people carry some level of risk when deciding who is eligible to receive

---

[1] Canadian Centre for Cybersecurity, "How to Identify Misinformation, Disinformation, and Malinformation," webpage, Communications Security Establishment, February 2022.

[2] D. J. Flyn, Brendan Nyhan, and Jason Reifler, "The Nature and Origins of Misperceptions: Understanding False and Unsupported Beliefs About Politics," *Advances in Political Psychology*, Vol. 38, Suppl. 1, 2017.

[3] We thank our internal reviewer, Ben Miller, for clarifying this point to the project team.

[4] Office of Personnel Management (OPM), *Standard Form 86: Questionnaire for National Security Positions*, November 2016.

a security clearance; the purpose of the SF-86 questions is to gather baseline information for further investigation related to these risk factors identified by the national security adjudicative guidelines from Security Executive Agent Directive (SEAD)-4.[5]

These guidelines for making a determination about security clearance eligibility are grounded in the *whole-person concept*, according to which adjudicators assess various factors that may arise in a background investigation of applicants and determine how those factors relate to the overall risk that the whole person presents. Some of the factors considered relate to potential security risks (e.g., foreign contacts, financial risks, or substance abuse), whereas other factors may mitigate existing risks (e.g., foreign contacts on approved U.S. government business, making a good-faith effort to repay overdue creditors, or satisfactory completion of a prescribed drug treatment program). The adjudicators evaluate these risks and mitigating factors to assess whether the risks are sufficiently low for individuals to be determined eligible to access classified information. There are aspects of this investigative and adjudicative process that could be confusing to applicants. This may cause some applicants to seek additional information and clarity from others about the process and whether details about their past might lead to long delays or even denial of a security clearance. Some applicants seek this information online—from sources of varying accuracy and reliability—potentially leading to misperceptions about the security clearance process in general.

Potential Consequences from Applicant Confusion

There are several potential consequences if current or prospective applicants are confused about the process for applying to receive a security clearance. First, misperceptions about what could lead to a clearance denial or revocation may deter people from even trying to apply for a security clearance. The process for receiving a clearance involves the weighting of risks and mitigating factors in the backgrounds of applicants. If these applicants primarily focus on risks, it could lead some to mistakenly believe that there is no chance for them to receive a clearance.

Second, misperceptions could lead some applicants to omit details about their lives on the SF-86 for fear of damaging their chances of getting a security clearance. Under certain conditions, these omissions could harm applicants more than merely being honest from the very beginning. They also could add to the time, effort, and costs by government investigators to fully assess the risks and mitigating factors within the backgrounds of applicants. Finally, misperceptions by applicants could lead some to have unnecessary anxiety while they wait for a decision about their application for a security clearance.

Report Outline

Chapter 1 outlines the background motivations for the rest of this report. In Chapter 2, we describe and analyze the accessibility of publicly available information from government (e.g., SEAD-4) and nongovernment (e.g., blogs) sources. In Chapter 3, we review conversations on three popular forums with communities that focused on discussions about the security clearance process in the United States. Chapter 4 summarizes findings and recommendations. In general, we found evidence that online information is anecdotal, is sometimes incomplete, and tends to focus on risk factors for clearance applicants. Such patterns may provide evidence for where the government could develop additional outreach to clarify confusion by the public.

---

[5] Office of the Director of National Intelligence (ODNI), *Security Executive Agent Directive 4: National Security Adjudicative Guidelines (SEAD-4)*, June 8, 2017a.

CHAPTER 2

Analysis of Publicly Available Online Government and Nongovernment Information

A prospective applicant searching for information regarding security clearances has several sources available to them, including searching online. These searches will lead applicants to find government sources, academic sources, and third-party websites that provide information on the process, rules, and guidelines involved in the application process. This chapter begins with a review of our approach to identifying different types of information, then presents some official online sources for this information, followed by a review of some unofficial online sources.

Reviewing the Landscape of Security Clearance Information

We examined official documents, official webpages, and unofficial sources covering three topics: security clearance applications, the adjudication process, and clearance requirements. We analyzed several types of documents: government directives, ancillary government documents, secondary sources such as academic websites or defense contractors, and media sources, including newspapers and podcasts. We used a convenience sample of online resources, meaning that our review is not representative of all online sources consumed by the public.

We identified relevant material from secondary and media sources by gathering a range of results found using general search terms related to security clearances, adjudication, and personnel vetting that were entered into Google.[1] We included sources that contained several paragraphs of information aimed specifically at clearance applicants—rather than other audiences, such as adjudicators or government contractor companies—from the first ten pages of results. This method led to 18 secondary sources: two videos, eight blogs, one report, and seven webpages. The same method produced 47 media sources: seven videos, 20 blogs, six magazine articles, six newspaper articles, two podcasts, and six other webpage results. All these results were used in the analysis in this chapter.

The first set of sources we analyzed consisted of official government documents online, produced by U.S. government agencies and serving as articulation of policy for the security clearance process. These documents included SEAD-4, SEAD-3, and the "Security Executive Agent Clarifying Guidance Concerning Marijuana" memorandum from ODNI.[2]

---

[1] These terms included "security clearance application," "security clearance advice," "apply for secret clearance," "security clearance myths," "security clearance faq," and "security clearance how to."

[2] ODNI, 2017a; ODNI, *Security Executive Agent Directive 3: Reporting Requirements for Personnel with Access to Classified Information or Who Hold a Sensitive Position*, June 12, 2017b. The ODNI memo clarifies the legal standing of marijuana usage for clearance holders. For brevity, this document will be abbreviated as the *ODNI marijuana memo* for the remainder of this report. ODNI, *Security Executive Agent Clarifying Guidance Concerning Marijuana for Agencies Conducting Adjudications of*

The second set of sources consisted of ancillary government online sources. These included secondary websites, such as USAJobs.gov, OPM website frequently asked questions (FAQs), Government Accountability Office (GAO) reports, and Congressional Research Service (CRS) reports.

The third set of sources we identified consisted of nongovernmental online resources from universities, defense contractors, and law firms. Examples of the first two included a university page on how to obtain government jobs and a defense contractor job application information page. The law firm websites covered clearance-related services, including pages on legal representation options for clearance applicants.[3] The sources also included public statements by select current and former government officials from congressional testimony, press releases, and news commentaries.

Finally, the fourth set of sources we identified consisted of online media sources that included magazines, newspapers, blogs, and specialty websites that tended to focus on specific guidelines, news related to policy changes, or government officials' statements. These were news articles on clearance updates, blog posts on clearance updates and news, and websites devoted to security clearance topics.[4]

Government Sources

Our analysis of government sources revealed that individual official documents are detailed, lengthy, and difficult to find and digest for many security clearance applicants but that these documents offer an authoritative source for the clearance process. Some sources and direct quotes from members of the security clearance community can offer clarity, although these are usually buried in lengthy articles or government documents. And as we discuss further below, some public figures have made inaccurate comments that are mistaken by media outlets as official statements and authoritative sources.

A member of the team scanned select official government documents for the main topics that the team identified as being related to the adjudication and application process and for information an applicant might want to know. Table 2.1 provides a full list of topics and categories that the team analyzed for the clearance adjudication process.

We identified the topics for analysis through an inductive approach to the existing documentation and sources. Specifically, we identified key themes according to their relevance to the clearance process. Working from a broad analysis across selected publicly available clearance information online, our team selected topics that were frequently discussed across the identified document categories. The rationale was that topics covered in several sources are likely to be of most interest to applicants.

Table 2.2 shows results from coding of the five sampled government documents. The table displays the types of information that were most prominent, as coded by a member of the research team. For a full list of the government documents assessed, see Appendix B.

We identified some variation in the amount of content that was prominent within each document. For example, the SEAD-4 covered eight of the 12 topics listed in Table 2.2,[5] while the CRS analysis, entitled

---

Persons Proposed for Eligibility for Access to Classified Information or Eligibility to Hold a Sensitive Position, ES 2021-01529, 2021.

[3] Lockheed Martin Corporation, "What Do I Need to Report?" webpage, 2021; Tully Rinckey, PLLC, "Security Clearance Lawyers," webpage, 2022.

[4] Philip Bump, "Trump Can Revoke Critics' Security Clearances If He Wants—But It Probably Wouldn't Change Much," *Washington Post*, July 23, 2018; Fox News Insider, "'Let the American Public Decide': Judge Nap Calls for Release of FISA Memo, Documents," January 29, 2018; ClearedJobs.Net, "Foreign National Contact and Your Security Clearance," YouTube video, May 16, 2014.

[5] ODNI, 2017a.

TABLE 2.1

Clearance Categories and Topics

Category	Analyzed Topics
Adjudication criteria	Job eligibility; types of clearances; objectivity and equality of the process
Measurements	Mentions of the importance of the truth; quality measures (trustworthiness, reliability, suitability, etc.); whole-person concept
Clearance guidelines	List of guidelines; detailed explanation of guideline components; existence of mitigating factors; explanation of marijuana guidance
Adjudication process	Stages of the adjudication process; an explanation of subsequent vetting and reporting processes once a clearance is granted, including Trusted Workforce 2.0, life event updates, and reinvestigation

SOURCES: Features information from selected online sources, such as ODNI, 2017a, and ODNI, 2021.

TABLE 2.2

Information Found in Official Government Online Sources

	Source				
Topic	SEAD-4	CRS	Bureau of Diplomatic Security	PAC Slides on Trusted Workforce 2.0	Office of Environment, Health, Safety and Security (EHSS)
Job eligibility	x	x	x		x
Types of clearances		x	x	x	x
Objectivity and equality of the process	x	x	x		
Mentions of the importance of the truth	x				x
Quality measures (trustworthiness, reliability, suitability, etc.)	x	x	x	x	
Whole-person concept	x			x	
List of guidelines	x	x			
Detailed explanation of guideline components	x				
Existence of mitigating factors	x	x	x		
Explanation of marijuana guidance				x	x
Stages of the adjudication process		x	x	x	x
An explanation of subsequent vetting and reporting processes			x	x	x

SOURCES: RAND analysis of listed online sources.

NOTE: The document from the CRS—which was created to provide useful information to members of Congress—is qualitatively different from the other documents that were created by responsible executive agencies (i.e., U.S. Department of State, the Performance Accountability Council [PAC]).

Security Clearance Process: Answers to Frequently Asked Questions, and the security clearances page of the Bureau of Diplomatic Security contained most of the topics in the Table 2.2.[6] These documents provided extensive and credible information on the whole-person concept and the application process more broadly. The SEAD-4 is the only document that we reviewed in Table 2.2 that provided a detailed explanation of guideline components, including the concerns and "conditions that could mitigate security concerns" for each guideline.[7]

The findings from this coding suggest that government documents share several common features that offer applicants a credible and comprehensive source of information. For example, the ODNI memo pertaining to marijuana use and security clearance adjudication states that "agencies are instructed that prior recreational marijuana use by an individual may be relevant to adjudications but not determinative."[8] This statement clarifies federal policy that previous marijuana use is not an absolute disqualifier for receiving a clearance but that adjudicators do take use of marijuana into consideration when assessing eligibility. As another example, to provide an understanding of the types of concerns and mitigating factors considered by adjudicators for each guideline, the SEAD-4 contains an itemized list of conditions that may mitigate risks that arise from these guidelines, such as the mitigating factor for Guideline E, Personal Conduct:

> The refusal or failure to cooperate, omission, or concealment was caused or significantly contributed to by advice of legal counsel or of a person with professional responsibilities for advising or instructing the individual specifically concerning security processes. Upon being made aware of the requirement to cooperate or provide the information, the individual cooperated fully and truthfully.[9]

This and several other mitigating factors for each guideline can provide applicants with an understanding of many of the factors adjudicators consider during the application process.

However, there are several challenges with the ways in which government sources present the information to potential clearance applicants. As discussed above, our analysis found that government sources are more difficult to understand compared with the other categories. To determine the difficulty of the evaluated sources, our team used the Flesch-Kincaid readability test included in Microsoft Word. This test is a commonly used tool to assess readability and states that documents should aim for a grade level between sixth and eighth and a minimum ease score of 50–60 percent.[10] This test measures the length of words and sentences to provide a grade-level and ease-of-reading score to all documents.[11] The grade-level score provides the grade in school an individual would have to complete in order to fully understand the text, where a grade-level score of 7.0 means a seventh grade student can comprehend the document. The reading ease score is ranked along a scale of 0 to 100, where higher scores indicate that the text is easier to read.

Each source was put into Word and reformatted before being run through the Flesch-Kincaid evaluation. In our sample set, government documents averaged a reading ease level of 11.0 and a grade level of 17.6 (e.g., 4.6 years post–high school). In contrast, the media sources had an average reading ease of 41.0 and a grade level of 12.3 (high school graduate); this places clearance media sources 5.3 grade levels lower than govern-

---

[6] Michelle D. Christensen, *Security Clearance Process: Answers to Frequently Asked Questions*, Congressional Research Service, October 7, 2016.

[7] ODNI, 2017a.

[8] ODNI marijuana memo, 2021.

[9] ODNI, 2021; ODNI, 2017a.

[10] Social Security Administration, "Program Operations Manual System (POMS)," webpage, September 28, 2015; Jerry L. Johns and Thomas E. Wheat, "Newspaper Readability: Two Crucial Factors," *Journal of Reading*, Vol. 27, No. 5, February 1984.

[11] Social Security Administration, 2015.

ment sources. While neither clearance topic media sources nor government sources reach the recommended levels, government sources scored as being harder to comprehend than media sources.[12]

Information sources may also be difficult to distinguish online, as default searches in search engines often mix results from newspapers and blogs with online government sources that may not fully represent the official government guidance and the process in its entirety. Results for the SEAD-4, SEAD-3, ODNI marijuana memo, OPM FAQ website, Defense Counterintelligence and Security Agency (DCSA) website, and ODNI website were not listed on the first few pages of search results about security clearances in general unless the specific titles of the documents were added to the searches. As noted by multiple studies, search engine users often click only on links on the first page of results, with between 71 percent and 92 percent of search results clicked on the first page.[13] Therefore, applicants are likely to focus on the first few pages of search engine results, and, as a result, authoritative sources may not be the sources most readily used by applicants.

While official government resources are a good online source of official and accurate information, they may be difficult to find and understand. These challenges with governmental sources may lead applicants to look to more easily consumable nongovernment sources to answer their questions.

Nongovernment Sources

Information on the security clearance process can also come from a variety of online sources apart from official government documents and sources. Those we reviewed include university job sites, defense contractor websites, law firms, magazines, news sites, and specialty websites. Most of these sources emphasize the importance of telling the truth on the SF-86 and throughout the security clearance process. Additionally, most of these sources provide true or somewhat true information, although the information may be oversimplified, which can lead to misperceptions by applicants.[14] However, as stated above, these documents are generally easier to understand compared with government sources.

Nongovernment job sites, news sites, and specialty or trade online sources tend to offer applicants clear, simple language that is easy to read quickly and is often organized under short headings or subtopics to ease navigation. Furthermore, they tend to be listed early in search engine results, meaning they are more likely to be read by prospective applicants.[15] Examples we found are several popular clearance-related blog posts that emphasize the importance of telling the truth,[16] taking your time in completing the SF-86,[17] and confessing if you did tell a lie during the security clearance process.[18]

---

[12] Accessible documents are important because security clearance applicants come from extremely varied educational backgrounds, and many cleared positions are available to high school graduates. Lindy Kyzer, "Top 10 Security Clearance Jobs That Don't Require a College Degree," *Clearance Jobs*, September 20, 2012.

[13] Additionally, the No. 1 result on Google has been reported to account for 34 percent of organic traffic across users. Owen Fay, "Value of #1 Position on Google for Traffic," webpage, Poll the People, May 6, 2022.

[14] For example, one magazine article quoted John Wojcik, listed as a manager of security and safety for a Department of Defense contractor, who "suggests you find out from human resources what the disqualifiers are before you quit your current job. 'You don't want to quit a good job only to find out that you are not eligible for clearance because you have relatives that live in another country,' he said."

[15] In the Google search engine, search results are listed according to an algorithm-based analysis of relevance (Google, "About Google Patents: Search Results Page," webpage, 2022).

[16] Marko Hakamaa, "Why You Should Tell the Truth About Why You Left a Job," blog post, Security Clearance Jobs, February 28, 2017.

[17] Brynn Mahnke, "Don't Get Denied: 5 Tips for Filling Out Your SF-86," *Clearance Jobs*, March 31, 2022.

[18] Katie Keller, "How to Overcome a Lie on the SF-86," *Clearance Jobs*, April 30, 2022.

However, several nongovernment sites, such as blogs and those for government contractors, tend to be overly specialized or focused on a single issue, such as IT-related risks or addressing foreign travel questions. Another concern with using the information from these sites is that the information is sometimes dated and not updated, whereas the government often removes earlier versions of outdated documents (or marks them as earlier versions) from online sources, making the most up-to-date information more easily available.[19] The government periodically updates such documents as the adjudicative guidelines and the SF-86, especially during the implementation of larger initiatives. For example, the government may update information released about Trusted Workforce 2.0 (a security clearance reform and modernization effort currently underway that we describe later in this report) that may not always be up to date on some nongovernment websites. So, if an applicant is searching on a particular topic, it becomes imperative that they note the date of the blog, website, or news article to understand how current and accurate the information may be.

One notable example of the potential for oversimplification—and applicant confusion as a result—appeared during our sampling of law firm websites that focused on potential risks in the clearance process. Our analysis reviewed 14 law firm websites, which appeared to emphasize the parts of the clearance process that are most arduous or potentially confusing, or they focused disproportionately on the risks that could exclude applicants—emphasizing why their legal services are needed to navigate the process. Some of the sources we reviewed warned that applicants with previous complications may struggle to receive a clearance. Some of the law firms sampled during our analysis included what might be perceived as sensational language to describe risks and the process. For example, one law office highlighted that "the road to a security clearance is filled with danger and opportunities for mistakes."[20] Other sources we examined suggested that filing for bankruptcy, adopting a child from overseas, traveling abroad, prior drug use, or an accusation of criminal activity might lead to a security clearance denial.[21] These warnings are not necessarily incorrect, but we note that they could lead some to attend to the risks more than mitigating factors.

In short, the materials produced by some law firms, in the form of informational videos, books, or web pages, tended to focus on all the possible pitfalls in the clearance process, with far less focus on the mitigating factors and the whole-person concept of adjudications. Interestingly, during the 2017 fiscal year, the National Counterintelligence and Security Center (NCSC) reported that an average of just 1.94 percent of security clearance applications were denied across ten reviewed agencies.[22]

Statements from Current and Former Government Officials

Several government officials whose work relates to the security clearance process have made public statements regarding the clearance process. Charles Allen—a credible source on these topics, having served in a number of related national security positions, including as Under Secretary of Homeland Security for Intelligence and Analysis—has provided congressional testimonies, written personal articles, and conducted inter-

---

[19] Several notable sources were from years earlier, including 2018, 2016, and 2012 (Rebecca Koenig, "What You Need to Know About Getting a Security Clearance," *U.S. News*, November 12, 2018; Rhoda Smackum, "Five Myths About Security Clearances for Federal Jobs," *Career Services Connection*, University of Maryland Global Campus, 2016; Ziran Zhang, *Security Clearance Denied: The Most Common Pitfalls for Security Clearance Applications*, Burnham & Gorokhov, PLLC, 2012).

[20] TheeClients, "Security Clearance Denial Security Application Mistakes," YouTube video, October 11, 2012; see also Claery & Hammond, LLP, "Security Clearance Disqualifiers," blog post, October 16, 2020.

[21] Alan Edmunds, "Security Clearance Denial | Foreign Influence | Foreign Preference," YouTube video, June 28, 2013; ClearedJobs.Net, 2014; Cara O'Neill, "Will Bankruptcy Affect My Military Security Clearance?" Nolo, undated; Lacey Langford, "What to Know About Security Clearances and Your Money," webpage, March 23, 2021.

[22] NCSC, *Fiscal Year 2017 Annual Report on Security Clearance Determinations*, 2018.

views regarding reforming the adjudication process, issues with the length of the process, clarification on the ODNI marijuana memo, and reforms for techniques that might be considered antiquated.[23]

Bill Evanina, another credible and authoritative source as former head of the ODNI's NCSC, offered congressional testimony and interviews in his official capacity regarding changes to the security clearance process over time, including Trusted Workforce 2.0 implementation.[24] Finally, Bill Lietzau, the current director of the DCSA as of the time of writing, has conducted interviews and authored articles regarding specifics of the SF-86, the adjudication process, and the whole-person concept.[25] While these and other members of the security clearance community have provided credible and accurate information, their statements are often buried in lengthy congressional hearings, interviews, or articles that make identification of the relevant information difficult without specifically querying on the names of the individuals themselves. The information in these sources may not always be easily consumable or comprehensible for prospective applicants.

Conclusion

This chapter presents a review and analysis of select government and nongovernment online sources pertaining to security clearances. This review provides a snapshot of available information, but it is not representative of all available content that the public may consume online. We find that government documents offer the most accurate information, but these sources tend to be detailed and could be difficult to comprehend, which may present challenges to the average reader in understanding the ins and outs of the process; these official documents can also be challenging to locate.[26] Most unofficial sources that we reviewed are easier to understand by an estimated five grade levels and emphasize the importance of being truthful throughout the process—but they are frequently either focused on a single topic or subset of topics related to security clearances, or oversimplify aspects of the security clearance process, which can lead to misperceptions by applicants.

---

[23] Charles E. Allen, *Statement of Assistant Secretary Charles E. Allen to the Subcommittee on Intelligence, Information Sharing, and Terrorism Risk Assessment*, House of Representatives Homeland Security Committee, 2007; Charles E. Allen, "Cannabis and Clearances: Unnecessarily Weeding Out Applicants," Clearance Jobs, July 22, 2020; C-SPAN, "Security Clearance Process," December 7, 2015.

[24] William Evanina, "Statement for the Record of NCSC Director Evanina for SSCI Hearing on Security Clearance Reform," National Counterintelligence and Security Center, 2020.

[25] Nicole Ogrysko, "Industry Urges DCSA to Accelerate Security Clearance Transformation Efforts," Federal News Network, May 27, 2021; Jane Edwards, *Bill Lietzau: DCSA Adds More Mission Areas to Advance Security Clearance Transformation*, ExecutiveGov, November 20, 2020.

[26] As shown by the U.S. Digital Service (USDS), government websites and documents can present challenges for certain consumers to use effectively (USDS, "An Inside Look at USDS," blog post, 2022).

CHAPTER 3

Analysis of Information Shared in Online Discussions About the Security Clearance Process

The previous chapter identified some of the official and unofficial information online that users may find with a simple web search. This chapter examines online communities for the type of information that may exist. In consultation with PAC, we focused on three popular online platforms with communities dedicated to the discussion of security clearance in the United States: Reddit, Federalsoup, and Clearancejobsblog. Most posts in our analysis appeared to be written based on anecdotal information, making it difficult for us to assess the veracity of claims made in posts. This analysis did allow us to identify what topics were of concern for users on these forums. This chapter describes our methodological approach, then presents our analysis of results followed by our conclusions.

Methodological Approach

We developed a three-step approach to analyze social media data in this study. Figure 3.1 displays each of these steps. First, we identified social media platforms with communities in which the U.S. security clearance process was both a salient and an enduring topic of discussion. For this analysis, we broadly defined social media by three features of platforms:[1] if they have user-generated content as a focal point of the platform, if users have the option to construct profiles for themselves, and if the platform allows users to interact with each other over time.

After consulting with the sponsor and subject-matter experts at RAND, we focused on three platforms that are home to communities explicitly focused on discussion of the security clearance process in the United States:

1. Reddit.com
2. Federalsoup.com
3. Clearancejobsblog.com

FIGURE 3.1
Analysis Plan for Social Media Data

---

[1]   Danah M. Boyd, "Social Network Sites as Networked Publics: Affordances, Dynamics, and Implications," in Zizi Papacharissi, ed., *Networked Self: Identity, Community, and Culture on Social Network Sites*, Routledge, 2010. In this report, we treat online discussion boards as a social media platform.

Second, within these platforms, we identified communities that are dedicated to discussing the security clearance process. For example, the subreddit r/SecurityClearance specifically states that it is "A place to ask questions and share advice about the security clearance process."[2] The "Security Clearance" section of Federalsoup.com states, "This area will allow those that have clearances [to] offer advice and suggestions to those inquiring about clearances or upgrading their clearances."[3] Finally, the forum for Clearancejobsblog.com states, "This blog is sponsored by ClearanceJobs.com, the largest security-cleared career network, specializes [sic] in defense jobs for professionals with federal security clearances."[4]

Within each of the platforms in our sample, we queried threads that focused on the following security-clearance communities:[5]

- r/SecurityClearance subreddit on Reddit.com[6]
- the "Security Clearance" cluster of threads from the forum on Federalsoup.com[7]
- the discussion board from Clearancejobsblog.com.[8]

We developed a tool to query years of posts from communities from each of the above social media platforms. We note that the topics discussed may vary by platform and over time based on a variety of factors related to the security clearance process (e.g., global pandemic, historic backlog, security risks). For the r/SecurityClearance subreddit, we queried 24,306 posts from January 1, 2017, until December 31, 2019. For the "Security Clearance" cluster of threads from the forum on Federalsoup.com, we queried 4,846 posts during the previous 12 years from the date of collection in January 2022.[9] For the discussion board from Clearancejobsblog.com, we queried 3,500 posts from January 10, 2017, to January 10, 2022.

Third, we applied an automated topic modeling tool that identified themes that were frequently discussed within these communities.[10] A *topic model* is a statistical model for discovering abstract *topics* in a collection of documents using natural language processing. Topic models estimate the probability of features that exist within a given document. These models organize text and gain insight into extensive collections of

---

[2] Reddit, "r/SecurityClearance," 2022.

[3] Federal Soup, "Security Clearance," 2022.

[4] "About," webpage, *Clearance Jobs Security Blog*, undated.

[5] We note that each forum has its own set of policies for online behavior, norms for moderating content, and moderators. Our analysis is forum-specific and does not make comparisons *among* forums. The Reddit r/SecurityClearance forum has rules listed at Reddit, 2022; Federalsoup.com has community terms of use stated on its website; finally, Clearancejobsblog.com's forum has community guidelines posted at "Community Guidelines," webpage, *Clearance Jobs Security Blog*, 2016.

[6] Reddit, 2022. Reddit is an online platform where users can submit written posts and give up or down votes to other users' posts. This platform is organized by communities focused on specific topics of user interest (e.g., music, humor, investing, the U.S. military, security clearances, sports). For more information, see Josh Boyd, "What Is Reddit?" Brandwatch, February 28, 2018.

[7] Federal Soup, 2022.

[8] Clearance Jobs Security Discussion, Discuss portal, 2022.

[9] The time stamps for posts used by Federalsoup.com are less precise for content created from months or years in the past. For example, current content will say the number of days and months (e.g., 25 days ago) from the date that we originally queried these data. Posts from the distant past have more-imprecise time stamps (e.g., about a month ago or about a year ago).

[10] This analysis looks only at *what* users posted online, not *how* they communicated with each other. Thus, the content of a single post may not reflect the totality of the back-and-forth that exists within these communities. Future research should consider adding this additional layer of analysis.

unstructured text bodies, and this is the reason we decided to use such modeling to analyze the social media platforms.

Topic modeling is a technique for identifying and classifying semantic patterns in a corpus of text. In a particular document, models are able to find clusters of words that appear more or less frequently compared with all the other words in a document.[11] Clusters of similar words make up the topics generated by statistical techniques. Appendix A describes in more detail the topic modeling techniques that we applied to our dataset.

Key Topics of Discussion

In this section, we review the most-popular topics of discussion from each forum of interest. We then highlight these topics with select examples of posts to identify areas of confusion for these users.[12] The examples illustrate what we found in most of the posts—not only from Reddit, but across all three online communities: users asking clarifying questions about the clearance process and guidelines, and other users responding with their personal opinions and perspectives. These examples are presented separately from discussions of factuality. In the subsequent section, we discuss the challenge of determining the veracity of online comments and the extent to which online posts reference official government documents.

Reddit

We identified a total of 46 clusters of topics on Reddit, representing posts from the r/SecurityClearance subreddit between 2017 and 2019. Table 3.1 displays the top ten clusters based on frequency of posts.

This table shows that the most frequent cluster in our sample is deleted posts and accounts. Most of these posts are from Reddit accounts that were deleted for various reasons. For example, users may post content and then decide to delete the post later but keep their Reddit account. Or a user may create an account without personal identifiers for privacy reasons. Further, a Reddit moderator might have decided to remove a post because it was irrelevant to the topic of security clearances or inappropriate, but that would still allow a user to keep their account and generate posts on a later date. The overwhelming majority of deleted posts came from users who appeared to have posted content at one time, then later deleted their account. We found that 2,548 of these deleted Reddit posts appeared to meet this criterion, representing 99.9 percent of all deleted posts.

The second most-frequent set of clustered posts that our model found consists of posts in which users are responding to others, mostly thanking another user for a previous post. We identified 785 of these posts, representing 3 percent of posts in our samples.

Besides those two most-frequent clusters of posts, the next most-frequent set of clusters focused on risk factors, including drug use (559 posts), foreign contacts (542 posts), citizenship-related questions (514 posts), financial history (486 posts), and alcohol- and court-related charges (479 posts). Together, these clusters of posts represent 10.6 percent of all posts in our sample.

---

[11] Harsh Lal and Priyanshu Lal, "NLP Chatbot for Discharge Summaries," *Institute of Electrical and Electronics Engineers 2nd International Conference on Intelligent Communication and Computational Techniques*, September 2019.

[12] This chapter presents examples of posts throughout. The authors have made slight edits to some of these posts to make it easier for readers to understand the content. We omit the usernames to protect the privacy of these users.

TABLE 3.1

Most Frequent Topics from the r/SecurityClearance Subreddit

Description of Cluster	Most Frequent Words	Number of Posts
Deleted posts or accounts	Deleted, roasted, copied, restarted	2,582
Thanking previous posters	Thanks, luck, welcome, best	785
Drug use	Use, drug, marijuana, years, weed	559
Foreign contacts	Contact, concerns, foreign, performed	542
Citizenship	Citizenship, dual, passport, foreign, renounce, country	514
Financial history	Debt, credit, pay, payments financials, debts, bankruptcy	486
Alcohol and court charges	Alcohol, charged, misdemeanor, court, drinking, felony, convicted	479
Background investigation process	Investigation, months, adjudication	442
Foreign travel or family contacts	Relatives, family, foreign, contact, travel	354
Military/Department of Defense questions	DoD, military, security, contact, officer	351

SOURCE: RAND analysis of the r/SecurityClearance Subreddit.

NOTE: DoD = U.S. Department of Defense. Results are from 24,306 available posts created between January 1, 2017, and December 31, 2019. Reddit labels posts from accounts that were deleted as "deleted," while deleted posts from existing accounts had content listed that often was banter between users (e.g., *roasted*).

Examples of Reddit Posts

To illustrate areas of confusion by online users from the r/SecurityClearance subreddit, we present three example posts that discuss drug use, foreign contacts, and citizenship-related questions. The first example is a response to a post by a user who claimed to be a senior in college and said that they accepted an offer from a defense department contractor. They stated that they had experimented with various drugs in college, including marijuana, ecstasy, acid, cocaine, and Adderall, but claimed to have stopped consuming drugs about a month prior to the post. Their post asked r/SecurityClearance about their chances of getting a clearance and whether their prior drug use could be mitigated. One user responded with this advice:

> I don't think you have any chance of getting a clearance right now. [T]he good news is drug use can be mitigated over time—and the fact it was experimental use—you'll need about a year for the marijuana use and probably a few years for the rest of the illegal drugs misuse of prescription drugs.

The second example is a post on foreign contacts in which a user raised concerns about distant family members who are Chinese citizens and whether occasional interactions with them during the holidays would be considered a significant risk factor:

> [I'm] not advertising for this guy or anything, but just an article I came across seeing as I am in a similar position. I have aunts [and] cousins who are foreign Chinese citizens whom I talk to very briefly during holiday times per year. [It] seems like even military service—and longtime citizenship [sic]—doesn't even help for people in cases like mine. [A]ny thoughts [or] discussion?

Finally, below is an example of a post that our model classified as a topic about citizenship, in which the user has a passport from a South American country but notes limited experiences in the country:

> The foreign passport is with a country in South America. Let's just leave it at that. I was never asked to renounce or turn over the foreign passport. I did disclose very thoroughly that I have no bank accounts in that country no recent travel to that country no intention of every living there \(although I once did\) [and have] no military service or voting there etc.

Federal Soup

We applied our classification model to the 4,846 posts that we queried from the "Security Clearance" cluster of threads on the forum of Federalsoup.com from 2010 through 2022.[13] Table 3.2 lists the top ten clusters by frequency of posts: These posts represent 40.1 percent of all posts from this sample. We found that most of the top clusters in our sample had posts that focused on the security clearance process, including questions about background investigations, personal background history, public trust clearance, SF-86, the adjudication process, or the general clearance process.

Table 3.2 shows that clusters of process-related questions (background investigation process, public trust clearance process, SF-86 questions, secret clearance process, adjudication process, general security clearance process) accounted for an estimated 1,314 posts in our sample. The other clusters we identified focused on risks, including 261 posts related to personal background history, 152 posts about employment history, 151 posts about foreign travel or contacts, and 89 posts about prior criminal records.

---

[13] On Federalsoup.com, some past posts did not display a specific date, but, instead, the dates were marked in more-general terms (e.g., four months ago or six years ago).

TABLE 3.2
Most Frequent Topics from Relevant Posts on Federalsoup.com

Description of Cluster	Most Frequent Words	Number of Posts
Background investigation process	Background, investigation, investigator, check, questions	308
Personal background history	Personnel, question, process, security, clearance, help	261
Public trust clearance process	Trust, public, risk, moderate, clearance	241
SF-86 questions	SF, residence, family, relatives, members, foreign, landlord	212
Secret clearance process	Secret, top, clearance, granted, interim, question, waiting	207
Adjudication process	Adjudication, process, adjudicators, time, long, question	192
General security clearance process	Security, clearance, questions, process	154
Employment history	Employment, job, employer, years, fired, new, current	152
Foreign travel or contacts	Foreign, contacts, spouse, travel, influence, marriage	151

Table 3.2—Continued

Description of Cluster	Most Frequent Words	Number of Posts
Prior Criminal Records	Arrest, criminal, traffic, felony, probation, misdemeanor	89

SOURCE: RAND analysis of the "Security Clearance" cluster of threads from the forum on Federalsoup.com.

NOTE: Results are from 4,846 available posts created in the past 12 years.

Examples of Federal Soup Posts

To illustrate areas of confusion by online users from Federalsoup.com, we present three example posts that discuss the background investigation process, personal background history, and the public trust clearance process.

Below is a post that our model classified as part of the background investigation process. This post is by a user asking about the role of past background investigations on current ones for a Secret clearance:

> I received favorable adjudication for a NCS [Noncritical-Sensitive]/Moderate Risk background investigation (Tier 3) for a summer position a few months ago but didn't receive a Secret Clearance since the position didn't require me to have it. I'm no longer at the agency. If I needed to get a Secret Clearance in the near future, is it possible that the results of my Tier 3 investigation could be used to simply grant me the clearance without having to go through the investigation process again? I know that I never received a Secret Clearance, but I have read that NCS/Moderate Risk positions and Secret Clearance positions utilize the same type of investigation.

The second example is a post that our model classified as related to personal background, which largely relates to individuals' experiences during the process. This post gives advice on how best to present intimate or personal details during the process:

> It doesn't need to be an arduous or stressful process. Keep intimate/personal details to a minimum. Being vague about why 'you' want to cross over isn't a bad thing.

Our third example is a post that our model classified as related to the public trust clearance process. In this example, a user is discussing the time frame it takes to receive a decision on this type of clearance when there are issues surrounding foreign contacts and dual citizenship:

> Public Trust is a 3–6 month process. Clarification on the status of the "clearance" could be pursued with the assistance of the Congressional representative. Highly unlikely further correspondences are forthcoming from the hiring manager or human resources or security.

> Regardless, errors in hiring aren't out of the question. Setting the paperwork to the side for 12 months could be one alternative to address error in hiring. Little recourse until receipt of the final offer.

Clearance Jobs Blog

Finally, we applied our topic model to 3,500 posts that we queried from the website Clearancejobsblog.com between 2017 and 2022. Again, our model identified clusters of posts, we ranked these clusters by the frequency of posts, and then we manually classified the topics based on the frequency of keywords within each cluster. Table 3.3 shows the top clusters from our model. As with our other findings, the most popular clus-

TABLE 3.3

Most Frequent Topics from Relevant Posts on Clearancejobsblog.com

Description of Cluster	Most Frequent Words	Number of Posts
TS/SCI or Polygraph Clearance Process	TS, SCI, poly, timeline, clearance, reinvestigation	197
Employment History	Employment, employer, job, jobs, SF, contractor, clearance, notice	175
Drug Use	Drug, use, usage, alcohol, marijuana, SF, cannabis, past	151
Public Trust Clearance Process	Trust, public, tier, risk, clearance, SF, question	149
SF-86 Questions	SF, section, question, form, filled, submitted, police, question	147
Foreign Contact	Foreign, citizenship, national, contacts, dual, naturalized, travel, passport, contact	127
Adjudication Process	Adjudication, question, background, security	108
Investigation Process	Security, investigation, question, process	104

Table 3.3—Continued

Description of Cluster	Most Frequent Words	Number of Posts
Security Clearance Denial	Suitability, denial, denied, appeal, determination, fitness	98
Military/DoD Questions	Military, commander, defense, army	82

SOURCE: RAND analysis of the Clearancejobsblog.com discussion board.

NOTE: This is a simple random sample of 200 posts from 3,500 available posts from January 10, 2017, to January 10, 2022.

ters of posts primarily focused on process (e.g., the Top Secret[TS]/Sensitive Compartmented Information [SCI] or Polygraph Clearance Process, Adjudication Process, or Investigation Process) or specific risks (e.g., Employment History, Drug Use, Foreign Contacts).

Examples of Clearance Jobs Blog Posts

This subsection displays some examples to describe areas of confusion that users raised on the Clearancejobsblog.com forum. The cluster with the largest number of posts is one related to TS/SCI or polygraph. To illustrate this confusion, in the following post, a user is asking about their level of clearance:

> why would both FSO's [Foreign Service Officers] see two different results about my clearance? As I stand now I'm unaware if I have a TS/SCI or Secret and this has frozen me from actively searching opportunities. Is there any cause for this confusion based on how I'm searched in JPAS [Joint Personnel Adjudication System] or is there something in writing and details I'm missing?

This second example post relates to employment history; the user is asking about a tentative job offer as they fill out the SF-86:

> First time applicant here. Does anyone add the tentative offer job that is the reason for the SF-86 as one of the entries under section 13? I know that all others and the current full time job need to be added. Thanks.

Finally, a third example post relates to drug use and the challenge of anticipating what an adjudicator thinks without having complete information about an applicant:

> It is hard to specify what an adjudicator thinks without seeing the whole case we shy away from that. What does stick out for me is that you are fully aware that drug use is prohibited while possessing a security clearance.

Analyzing the Veracity of Online Posts

Two members of the team reviewed a random sample of 20 posts from the most popular clusters described in the above sections. The coders independently reviewed and coded the same sample of posts for accuracy by cross-referencing the posts to guidance from the SEAD-4.[14] The coders were in complete agreement that all the posts contained partial truths. This result shows the limitations in correctly determining the veracity of posts where there is limited information about the user, their background, and past experiences. Put simply, posts with limited information—especially details about individual experiences—are difficult to assess as correct or incorrect. Thus, we concluded that the results from this analysis cannot assess the veracity of online posts without additional details.

Our analysis turned to examining the number of posts that referenced external resources. Table 3.4 displays the frequency of URLs (i.e., frequency of text that references "http" or "www") and URLs referencing official government websites (i.e., posts that contained linked ".gov") for each platform.

We found a small percentage of references to external websites and an even smaller percentage of references linking to official government websites. For example, we identified content of external websites 980 times in our sample of Reddit posts, representing 0.10 percent of all words in this sample. Further, we identified 72 links to government resources that people posted on Reddit, representing 0.01 percent of all words in that sample of posts.

For Federal Soup, we identified 204 times that users referenced an external URL, representing 0.34 percent of all words in this sample. We identified only 12 posts that included government URLs, representing 0.02 percent of all words in our sample. Finally, we identified 95 times that external URLs were posted on Clearancejobsblog.com, representing 0.52 percent of all words in that sample of posts. We found seven times that a government URL was posted, representing 0.04 percent of words in this sample.

Conclusion

This chapter applies topic modeling to three online communities that are dedicated to discussing the security clearance process in the United States. Results show that most posts focused on the security clearance process or risk factors. We displayed some examples to showcase what users were discussing. These posts generally asked clarifying questions about applying for a security clearance, focused on individual experiences, and relied on anecdotal evidence. The team attempted to code these posts based on the veracity of statements, but this could not be done because of the limited information contained in these individual posts. We then examined the number of times that users posted links to external sources, finding that a small fraction of posts included URLs in general, and fewer included links to government URLs.

TABLE 3.4

Frequency of URLs and Government URLs, by Platform

	Reddit	%	Federal Soup	%	Clearance Jobs Blog	%
URLs	980	0.10	204	0.34	95	0.52
.gov URLs	72	0.01	12	0.02	7	0.04

SOURCE: RAND analysis of the r/SecurityClearance subreddit, Federalsoup.com, and Clearancejobsblog.com.

NOTE: Results are from 967,701 words in 24,306 available posts created between January 1, 2017, and December 31, 2019, from the r/SecurityClearance subreddit; 59,208 words from 4,846 available posts created in the past 12 years from Federalsoup.com; and 18,101 words from 3,500 available posts from January 10, 2017, to January 10, 2022, from Clearancejobsblog.com.

---

[14] ODNI, 2017a.

CHAPTER 4

Conclusion and Recommendations

The process of applying for and receiving a security clearance can seem opaque, which is one reason why some individuals seek clarity from sources online about the process. However, not all information available online is correct or easily consumable. In this report, the authors looked to identify where people discuss or post about security clearance–related topics online, what topics are covered, and areas in which these popular discussions or website resources contain falsehoods and misperceptions. To accomplish this, we queried and analyzed posts from three popular social media communities that cater to discussions about the security clearance process and reviewed online sources from government and nongovernment websites. The steps we took in this analysis led us to three conclusions and three sets of recommendations.

First, we reviewed official government documents about the security clearance process as well as third-party resources. While the government documents were detailed and comprehensive, they could be difficult for members of the public to fully comprehend. We also reviewed unofficial sources (e.g., university job websites, law firms, magazine and news websites) that, in general, provided clearer and easier-to-read information, though they often focused on specific topics. Again, some of this information from unofficial sources was not necessarily false, but it was not fully accurate either, nor always comprehensive. In some cases, the seemingly clarifying information related to the security clearance process provided by such sources can be in the form of anecdotes that may increase misperceptions among the general public. This leads us to the following recommendation:

Recommendation 1: We recommend that the federal government develop and release more accessible, easy-to-understand content that explains the nuances of the security clearance process and includes explanations about the whole-person concept, risk factors, and factors that may mitigate risks.

This recommendation could include FAQ documents that address some of the more predominant questions (and misperceptions) that individuals have as they go through the security clearance process. Also, we developed an analysis plan (Figure 3.1) and applied a set of tools that the government could use to assess the types of topics that could lead to misperceptions online. Using a simple tool for querying data from Reddit, Clearancejobsblog.com, and Federalsoup.com, and then using Google's Bidirectional Encoder Representations from Transformers (BERT) model,[1] we were able to classify clusters of online posts according to their content. Using this approach, we found specific topics that users were posting about online. Most posts in our sample focused on process-related topics or risk factors. Based on these results, we suggest the government avoid attempting to determine the accuracy of online comments that are often made without sufficient context to assess their veracity fully and objectively. However, these comments still provide valuable insight into the aspects of the security clearance process that are concerning or confusing people. This leads us to our second recommendation.

Recommendation 2: We recommend that the federal government periodically assess online information about the security clearance process to understand what information and misperceptions should be addressed.

---

[1] Python Package Index, "bert-embedding 1.0.1," webpage, 2019.

We found that coding posts based on assessments of truth or falsehood did not produce meaningful results. Given the anecdotal nature of these online posts and the limited information contained within them, it was challenging to accurately assess whether a post was false. In general, we found that most posts in our sample contained some degree of accurate information. We then focused on assessing the features of these posts that may lead to misperceptions. Results showed that a relatively small percentage of content linked to official government websites, but a higher percentage did link to nongovernment online sources. This leads us to our third recommendation.

Recommendation 3a: We recommend that the federal government consider an effort to conduct targeted outreach on some of these online forums that directs users to more official sources.

This recommendation should be subject to a cost-benefit analysis for topics that are of highest priority to federal agencies.

Recommendation 3b: We recommend that the federal government evaluate the effectiveness of outreach on popular online forums.

We note that such evaluations may include interventions that use specific (anonymized) examples from people, frequent questions answered by security officials, or individual experiences of actual clearance applicants.

Looking Ahead: A Note on Trusted Workforce 2.0

Most of the data and information that we found online for this study was focused on the way security clearances traditionally have been processed over the past few decades. However, as mentioned earlier in this report, the federal government is undertaking a significant transformation effort related to personnel vetting with implementation of the Trusted Workforce 2.0 initiative. This includes an updated initial vetting process and anticipated reduction of timelines for onboarding, continuous vetting with internal and external data monitoring once an employee or contractor is granted clearance, and a number of other measures.[2] With such significant changes to the security clearance process underway and forthcoming, there are likely to be new questions from applicants, employees, and contractors about what this all means as more about Trusted Workforce 2.0 becomes public, including questions about what is changing, what continuous vetting entails, and how the transforming system could affect their individual circumstances. Assumptions, misperceptions, and even false narratives are possible, such as continuous vetting being perceived by some as invasive surveillance and "Big Brother" always watching or concerns about how machine learning and artificial intelligence capabilities may be brought to bear and how reliable they are. Getting ahead of potential misperceptions now with factual information from authoritative government sources—presented in a clear and accessible way (as mentioned in Recommendation 1)—can help reduce confusion and misperceptions, particularly for would-be applicants seeking a position in the national security workforce.

---

[2] DCSA, "Trusted Workforce 2.0 and Continuous Vetting," webpage, 2022.

Methodological Details

In this appendix, we review some of the methodological details for the topic models that we discussed in Chapter 2.[1] These were unsupervised learning models that analyze the distribution of topics in any given corpus. Using this technique, we define any topic by the frequency of the repeated terms, and the algorithm generates a probability distribution for each topic in the text corpus.

Bidirectional Encoder Representations from Transformers Topic (BERTopic), a topical modeling technique that utilizes BERT embeddings,[2] uses two Uniform Manifold Approximation and Projection (UMAP)[3] and Hierarchical Density-Based Spatial Clustering of Applications with Noise (HDBSCAN)[4] algorithms through the following three steps:

1. **Sentence embedding.** In this step, we generated embeddings for the Reddit posts to provide a numerical representation in the format of vectors.[5] For this step, we used a pretrained transformer.
2. **Semantically similar sentence clusters.** We used the UMAP algorithm to reduce the dimensionality of the embedding vectors. *Cosine similarity*,[6] a metric used to measure the similarity of the documents, was used to find the distance between the various data points.
3. **Topic representation using class-based term frequency–inverse document frequency.**[7] We performed a clustering technique using the HDBSCAN algorithm to find the similarity between the documents in the semantic space to produce a unique topic. The team decided the number of topics, which was top-ten listed in Tables 3.1, 3.2, and 3.3, based on their experience with the subject.

The datasets we used were collected from three public platforms by a data-querying technique using Python.[8] The team excluded the "noise" in the collected text and preprocessed the data by removing the stop words, punctuations, and emojis. Also, we removed the platform-related noise like user hashtags, usernames, and mentions. Further, as part of preprocessing the data, we conducted *stemming*, removing any suffixes or prefixes from the words.

---

[1] Ike Vayansky and Sathish A. P. Kumar, "A Review of Topic Modeling Methods," *Information Systems*, Vol. 94, December 2020.

[2] Python Package Index, 2019.

[3] "UMAP: Uniform Manifold Approximation and Projection for Dimension Reduction," webpage, 2018.

[4] HDBSCAN, "How HDBSCAN Works," webpage, 2016.

[5] For technical details on BERT, see Open AI, "Embeddings," webpage, undated.

[6] Faisal Rahutomo, Terukai Kitasuka, and Masayoshi Aritsugi, "Semantic Cosine Similarity," *7th International Student Conference on Advanced Science and Technology*, Vol. 4, No. 1, October 2012.

[7] Seyyed Mohammad Hossein Dadgar, Mohammad Shirzad Araghi, and Morteza Mastery Farahani, "A Novel Text Mining Approach Based on TF-IDF and Support Vector Machine for News Classification," *2016 IEEE International Conference on Engineering and Technology (ICETECH)*, March 2016.

[8] Richard Lawson, *Web Scraping with Python: Successfully Scrape Data from Any Website with the Power of Python*, Packt Publishing, 2015.

Full Government Source Document Table

There are two sets of government sources listed in Table B.1. The first set of sources consists of official government documents online, produced by U.S. government agencies and serving as articulation of policy for the security clearance process. These documents include SEAD-4, SEAD-3, and the ODNI marijuana memorandum.

The second set of sources consists of ancillary government online sources. These include secondary websites, such as USAJobs.gov, OPM website FAQs, GAO reports, and CRS reports. The sources also include public statements by current and former government officials from congressional testimony, press releases, and news commentaries.

Table B.1 shows that, for personnel-vetting policy and documents, the level and type of information vary widely across official government online sources and ancillary government online sources. Of the 14 government sources analyzed, nine mention job eligibility and the "need to know," the types of clearances, and continuous vetting. Eight sources discuss the stages of the application process, and seven sources discuss the measured qualities of an applicant. One source breaks down a detailed explanation of the guidelines, two sources emphasize the importance of the truth, and three sources list the guidelines or clarify the mitigating factors considered during the adjudication process. For example, the EHSS states that personnel considered "for access to classified information or special nuclear material (SNM) [must] meet national standards of honesty,"[1] while the CRS report highlights that "Adjudicators are also instructed to consider any conditions that could mitigate the associated security concerns."[2]

Topics included in the table pertain to information that an applicant may wish to be aware of before or during the application process. Topics were marked as discussed within the analyzed documents if they were mentioned by the source.

---

[1] EHSS, "Departmental Personnel Security FAQs," webpage, undated.

[2] Christensen, 2016.

TABLE B.1
Coding of Source Documents About the Security Clearance Process

Source	Process		Guidelines				Measurements			Adjudication Criteria		
	Explanation of Subsequent Vetting and Reporting Processes	Stages of Adjudication	Marijuana Guidance	Mitigating Factors	Explanation of Guideline Components	List of Guidelines	Whole-Person Concept	Quality Measures	Mentions Importance of the Truth	Objectivity and Equality of the Process	Types of Clearances	Job Eligibility
ODNI, 2017a (SEAD-4)				X	X	X	X	X	X	X	X	X
CRS		X		X		X		X		X	X	X
Bureau of Diplomatic Security	X	X		X				X		X	X	X
PAC Slides on Trusted Workforce 2.0	X	X	X				X	X			X	
EHSS	X	X	X						X		X	X
OPM website	X	X					X			X		X
DCSA website	X	X						X			X	X
U.S. Department of Agriculture	X	X									X	X
National Nuclear Security Administration	X	X	X					X				
USA Jobs								X			X	X
U.S. Small Business Administration		X				X					X	
ODNI, 2017b (SEAD-3)	X											X
ODNI marijuana memo			X				X			X		
ODNI website	X											

SOURCES: RAND coding of listed documents.

Abbreviations

BERT	Bidirectional Encoder Representations from Transformers
BERTopic	Bidirectional Encoder Representations from Transformers Topic
CRS	Congressional Research Service
DCSA	Defense Counterintelligence and Security Agency
DoD	U.S. Department of Defense
EHSS	Office of Environment, Health, Safety and Security
FAQ(s)	frequently asked question(s)
GAO	Government Accountability Office
HDBSCAN	Hierarchical Density-Based Spatial Clustering of Applications with Noise
NCSC	National Counterintelligence and Security Center
ODNI	Office of the Director of National Intelligence
OPM	Office of Personnel Management
PAC	Performance Accountability Council
SEAD	Security Executive Agent Directive
SF	Standard Form
TS/SCI	Top Secret/Sensitive Compartmented Information
UMAP	Uniform Manifold Approximation and Projection

References

"About," webpage, *Clearance Jobs Security Blog*, undated. As of December 13, 2022:
https://www.clearancejobsblog.com/about/

Allen, Charles E., *Statement of Assistant Secretary Charles E. Allen to the Subcommittee on Intelligence, Information Sharing, and Terrorism Risk Assessment*, House of Representatives Homeland Security Committee, 2007.

Allen, Charles E., "Cannabis and Clearances: Unnecessarily Weeding Out Applicants," Clearance Jobs, July 22, 2020.

Boyd, Danah M., "Social Network Sites as Networked Publics: Affordances, Dynamics, and Implications," in Zizi Papcharissi, ed., *Networked Self: Identity, Community, and Culture on Social Network Sites*, Routledge, 2010.

Boyd, Josh, "What Is Reddit?" Brandwatch, February 28, 2018. As of August 12, 2022:
https://www.brandwatch.com/blog/what-is-reddit-guide/

Bump, Philip, "Trump Can Revoke Critics' Security Clearances If He Wants—But It Probably Wouldn't Change Much," *Washington Post*, July 23, 2018.

Canadian Centre for Cybersecurity, "How to Identify Misinformation, Disinformation, and Malinformation," webpage, Communications Security Establishment, February 2022. As of December 12, 2022:
https://cyber.gc.ca/sites/default/files/cyber/2022-02/ITSAP-00-300-How-To-Identify-Misinformation_e.pdf

Christensen, Michelle D., *Security Clearance Process: Answers to Frequently Asked Questions*, Congressional Research Service, October 7, 2016.

Claery & Hammond, LLP, "Security Clearance Disqualifiers," blog post, October 16, 2020. As of December 9, 2022:
https://www.securityclearanceadvocates.com/blog/2020/october/security-clearance-disqualifiers/

Clearance Jobs Security Discussion, Discuss portal, 2022. As of December 9, 2022:
https://discuss.clearancejobsblog.com

ClearedJobs.Net, "Foreign National Contact and Your Security Clearance," YouTube video, May 16, 2014. As of December 9, 2022:
https://www.youtube.com/watch?v=Ixuetaf-OF4

"Community Guidelines," webpage, *Clearance Jobs Security Blog*, 2016.

C-SPAN, "Security Clearance Process," December 7, 2015. As of December 9, 2022:
https://www.c-span.org/video/?401648-1/discussion-security-clearance-protocols

Dadgar, Seyyed Mohammad Hossein, Mohammad Shirzad Araghi, and Morteza Mastery Farahani, "A Novel Text Mining Approach Based on TF-IDF and Support Vector Machine for News Classification," *2016 IEEE International Conference on Engineering and Technology (ICETECH)*, March 2016.

DCSA—*See* Defense Counterintelligence and Security Agency.

Defense Counterintelligence and Security Agency, "Trusted Workforce 2.0 and Continuous Vetting," webpage, 2022. As of December 9, 2022:
https://www.dcsa.mil/mc/pv/cv/

Edmunds, Alan, "Security Clearance Denial | Foreign Influence | Foreign Preference," YouTube video, June 28, 2013. As of December 9, 2022:
https://www.youtube.com/watch?v=kv4klf1LOjw

Edwards, Jane, "Bill Lietzau: DCSA Adds More Mission Areas to Advance Security Clearance Transformation," *ExecutiveGov*, November 20, 2020.

EHSS—*See* Office of Environment, Health, Safety and Security.

Evanina, William, "Statement for the Record of NCSC Director Evanina for SSCI Hearing on Security Clearance Reform," National Counterintelligence and Security Center, 2020.

Fay, Owen, "Value of #1 Position on Google for Traffic," webpage, Poll the People, May 6, 2022. As of December 9, 2022:
https://pollthepeople.app/the-value-of-google-result-positioning-3/

Federal Soup, "Security Clearance," 2022.

Flyn, D. J., Brendan Nyhan, and Jason Reifler, "The Nature and Origins of Misperceptions: Understanding False and Unsupported Beliefs About Politics," *Advances in Political Psychology*, Vol. 38, Suppl. 1, 2017.

Fox News Insider, "'Let the American Public Decide': Judge Nap Calls for Release of FISA Memo, Documents," January 29, 2018. As of December 9, 2022:
https://www.foxnews.com/video/5721662401001

Google, "About Google Patents: Search Results Page," webpage, 2022. As of December 9, 2022:
https://support.google.com/faqs/answer/7049588?hl=en

Hakamaa, Marko, "Why You Should Tell the Truth About Why You Left a Job," blog post, Security Clearance Jobs, February 28, 2017. As of August 2, 2022:
https://www.clearancejobsblog.com/why-you-should-tell-the-truth-about-why-you-left-a-job/

HDBSCAN, "How HDBSCAN Works," webpage, 2016. As of December 9, 2022:
https://hdbscan.readthedocs.io/en/latest/how_hdbscan_works.html

Johns, Jerry L., and Thomas E. Wheat, "Newspaper Readability: Two Crucial Factors," *Journal of Reading*, Vol. 27, No. 5, February 1984.

Keller, Katie, "How to Overcome a Lie on the SF-86," Clearance Jobs, April 30, 2022.

Koenig, Rebecca, "What You Need to Know About Getting a Security Clearance," *U.S. News*, November 12, 2018.

Kyzer, Lindy, "Top 10 Security Clearance Jobs That Don't Require a College Degree," Clearance Jobs, September 20, 2012.

Lal, Harsh, and Priyanshu Lal, "NLP Chatbot for Discharge Summaries," *Institute of Electrical and Electronics Engineers 2nd International Conference on Intelligent Communication and Computational Techniques*, September 2019.

Langford, Lacey, "What to Know About Security Clearances and Your Money," webpage, March 23, 2021. As of December 9, 2022:
https://laceylangford.com/security-clearances-and-money/

Lawson, Richard, *Web Scraping with Python: Successfully Scrape Data from Any Website with the Power of Python*, Packt Publishing, 2015.

Lockheed Martin Corporation, "What Do I Need to Report?" webpage, 2021. As of December 9, 2022:
https://www.lockheedmartin.com/en-us/employees/reportable.html

Mahnke, Brynn, "Don't Get Denied: 5 Tips for Filling Out Your SF-86," Clearance Jobs, March 31, 2022.

National Counterintelligence and Security Center, *Fiscal Year 2017 Annual Report on Security Clearance Determinations*, 2018.

NCSC—*See* National Counterintelligence and Security Center.

ODNI—*See* Office of the Director of National Intelligence.

Office of Environment, Health, Safety and Security, "Departmental Personnel Security FAQs," webpage, undated. As of December 9, 2022:
https://www.energy.gov/ehss/security-policy-guidance-reports/departmental-personnel-security-faqs

Office of Personnel Management, *Standard Form 86: Questionnaire for National Security Positions*, November 2016. As of July 28, 2022:
https://www.opm.gov/forms/pdf_fill/sf86.pdf

Office of the Director of National Intelligence, *Security Executive Agent Directive 4: National Security Adjudicative Guidelines (SEAD-4)*, June 8, 2017a.

Office of the Director of National Intelligence, *Security Executive Agent Directive 3: Reporting Requirements for Personnel with Access to Classified Information or Who Hold a Sensitive Position*, June 12, 2017b.

Office of the Director of National Intelligence, *Security Executive Agent Clarifying Guidance Concerning Marijuana for Agencies Conducting Adjudications of Persons Proposed for Eligibility for Access to Classified Information or Eligibility to Hold a Sensitive Position*, ES 2021-01529, 2021.

Ogrysko, Nicole, "Industry Urges DCSA to Accelerate Security Clearance Transformation Efforts," Federal News Network, May 27, 2021.

O'Neill, Cara, "Will Bankruptcy Affect My Military Security Clearance?" Nolo, undated.

Open AI, "Embeddings," webpage, undated. As of December 14, 2022:
https://beta.openai.com/docs/guides/embeddings/what-are-embeddings

Python Package Index, "bert-embedding 1.0.1," webpage, 2019. As of December 12, 2022:
https://pypi.org/project/bert-embedding/

Rahutomo, Faisal, Terukai Kitasuka, and Masayoshi Aritsugi, "Semantic Cosine Similarity," *7th International Student Conference on Advanced Science and Technology*, Vol. 4, No. 1, October 2012.

Reddit, "r/SecurityClearance," 2022. As of December 9, 2022:
https://www.reddit.com/r/SecurityClearance/

Smackum, Rhoda, "Five Myths About Security Clearances for Federal Jobs," *Career Services Connection*, University of Maryland Global Campus, 2016.

Social Security Administration, "Program Operations Manual System (POMS)," webpage, September 28, 2015. As of December 9, 2022:
https://secure.ssa.gov/poms.nsf/lnx/0910605105

TheeClients, "Security Clearance Denial Security Application Mistakes," YouTube video, October 11, 2012. As of December 12, 2022:
https://www.youtube.com/watch?v=cA_CqVsxOkk

Tully Rinckey, PLLC, "Security Clearance Lawyers," webpage, 2022. As of December 12, 2022:
https://www.tullylegal.com/legal-services/security-clearance-representation/

"UMAP: Uniform Manifold Approximation and Projection for Dimension Reduction," webpage, 2018. As of December 12, 2022:
https://umap-learn.readthedocs.io/en/latest/

U.S. Digital Service, "An Inside Look at USDS," blog post, 2022.

USDS—*See* U.S. Digital Service.

Vayansky, Ike, and Sathish A. P. Kumar, "A Review of Topic Modeling Methods," *Information Systems*, Vol. 94, December 2020.

Zhang, Ziran, *Security Clearance Denied: The Most Common Pitfalls for Security Clearance Applications*, Burnham & Gorokhov, PLLC, 2012.